102 Tweets

Social Media Update Ideas for Businesses & Nonprofits

by Tim Priebe

T&S™

102 Tweets
Social Media Update Ideas for Businesses & Nonprofits

Tim Priebe

ISBN: 978-0-692-20928-8

Author Contact
The author may be contacted at the following address:

T&S Web Design
PO Box 1478
Edmond, OK 73083

http://www.tandswebdesign.com
info@tandswebdesign.com
405-285-0348

Author's Forward

If you're like many others, you know that social media can be beneficial. You see other people using it for their business or nonprofit. But when it comes time for you to use it, you have no clue what to write about.

Simply put, you suffer from writer's block!

If that sounds like something that's frustrated you in the past, then this is the book for you!

This is not a book about an overall social media plan, best practices on social media sites like Twitter and Facebook, or how to build up your following.

Rather, it's a simple tool to overcome writer's block whenever you get it. Although we specifically talk about Twitter, and limit the sample updates to 140 characters, the ideas in this book can be applied to most social media websites.

So let's get to it!

#Tweet1

First Tweet

It may seem a little trite, but make sure you put something out there when you first sign up for Twitter, before you start following people. You're more likely to get people following you back if you do.

> **Golding Group** @GoldingGroup
>
> It all begins January 2nd, 2012....

#Tweet2

Prediction

Make a stand on what you think is going to happen in the future. It can be anything from a local sports team to a national news or industry news event.

RococosCrabCake @RococosCrabCake

@DanGordon prediction: @Lakers 88 @okcthunder 110 #ThunderUp

Jokes

Two Twitter accounts walk into a bar. One shares a tasteful joke, while the other just goes around promoting himself. Which one do you think people are going to pay any attention to?

T and S Web Design @tandswebdesign

For every action, there is an equal and opposite reaction, plus a social media overreaction.

#Tweet4

Shocking

Being shocking works for magazine covers, for the news, for articles... The list goes on. Say something shocking (but true) that your followers aren't expecting. If you include a link, your followers will be more likely to click on it than normal links.

Jay D. Parks CPA @jayparkscpa

If I don't give you a bang for your buck, you need to fire me, period. I should pay for myself as an investment, not an expense.

#Tweet5

Facts

Just because it's common knowledge for you, doesn't mean that it's common knowledge for someone else. Share some fact about your industry that's relevant to your target market, and your followers will appreciate it. Combine it with a question to get more interaction.

> **Taylor Richardson** @EliteInsOK
> "@ijournal: Insurer Loss Ratios High Oklahoma After Years of Storms bit.ly/1aULEZL " Since '07 the loss ratios for home ins are 133%

#Tweet6

Studies

Even better than sharing a tidbit of a fact is linking to an entire study that was done. It can be a new study, although old studies that are still relevant are fine as well. And be sure to briefly summarize the results in your tweet when you send out the link.

T and S Web Design @tandswebdesign
Wondering how effective social media really is at connecting businesses with their customers? Read this study. - ow.ly/gjwnA

#Tweet7

Short Lists

Have a short, helpful list? Trim it until it's down to the required 140 characters, then tweet it out! Lists are easy for people to read, and therefore popular.

> **Sandler Training OK** @SandlerOklahoma
> 3 ways to grow your business: Talk to more people, talk to better people, or have better conversations.

#Tweet8

How To

How to articles are extremely helpful to the do-it-yourselfers. You can share a full blown article you or someone else wrote. Or, if it's simple, just share the how to in the actual tweet.

Jay D. Parks CPA @jayparkscpa

Read how to identify the gaps in your situation. - ow.ly/ltlm8

#Tweet9

Entertaining

While being entertaining all the time won't help most organizations, some entertainment from time to time can definitely make you seem more human, and not like a stuffy, stuck up Twitter account. It will make you more personable, and therefore more approachable.

T and S Web Design @tandswebdesign
Angry Birds in Real Life: Angry Birds in real life, courtesy of the Orangites here at T&S. This was the last vid...
bit.ly/KahNhD

#Tweet10

Inspirational Quotes

Send out a quote or two! Nice and inspiring, they can make a great, quick update. If you're also posting on social media sites that use graphics, include a link to the person's Wikipedia page or their own website.

> **Sandler Training OK** @SandlerOklahoma
> "I attribute my success to this - I never gave or took any excuse." - Florence Nightingale

#Tweet11

Newsworthy Quotes

Like an inspirational quote, a newsworthy quote can make for a quick update. Just pull something that's relatively short from a news article, and make sure to link from the article. Make sure it stands well on its own. And if the source has a Twitter account, make sure to attribute that as well.

T and S Web Design @tandswebdesign

"It's easy to go down the path to where it gets too noisy too quickly." - Dick Costolo, CEO of Twitter - ow.ly/

#Tweet12

Book Quotes

Read a book recently that you loved, and you think your target market would benefit from? Find a section that's particularly good, and that fits in 140 characters and less. And if it's 110 characters or so after you include the attribution, go ahead and link to the book on Amazon as well.

> **Taylor Richardson** @EliteInsOK
> "Soon is not as good as now" - Seth Godin - ow.ly/mrIVJ

#Tweet13

Employee Quotes

If you're like more work places, your employees say funny things from time to time. If you're like my workplace, it's a constant stream of hilarity. Share the appropriate ones!

T and S Web Design @tandswebdesign

"I had a nightmare last night...I was designing a dynamic width website." - @littler4bbit

#Tweet14

Blog Articles You Wrote

If you pour work into writing new blog articles, make sure you take advantage of social media as a platform to share them. If your title is enticing and descriptive, you can just include it and the link. You can also try using a brief description before your link, or a direct excerpt.

Jay D. Parks CPA @jayparkscpa

Protect your family from identity theft with one simple step. - ow.ly/msc4m

#Tweet15

Your Old Blog Articles

Don't limit yourself to only using your latest blog articles. Scour the archives for articles that are still relevant today. And you can also share some that are great blasts from the past, providing some entertainment value even if the information isn't completely relevant any longer.

> **Golding Group** @GoldingGroup
> Looking Back: Blog post from 1 year ago today - New Client Announcement @Rococos @Rococo_NP

#Tweet16

Blog Articles By Others

Follow the blogs written by your clients, vendors, strategic partners, neighbors, and others. Then when they share something you think would benefit your audience, you can share it as well.

T and S Web Design @tandswebdesign

Concerned about SEO? Then Facebook and Twitter are extremely important. - ow.ly/mux0t

#Tweet17

Entire Blog

You don't have to limit your plug to a specific blog entry. If you think your target market will enjoy all the articles on a blog, plug the whole thing! If you've found an entirely new resource for your customers, they'll love it.

> **Golding Group** @GoldingGroup
> Make sure & check out the personal blogs of Golding Group partners @KyleGolding bit.ly/ffHa2q & @FeliciteMoorman bit.ly/yx0CnA

#Tweet18

Videos by You

Have you put time, effort, and maybe even money into creating a video? Don't just share it on your website, make sure to promote it through your social media channels as well.

T and S Web Design @tandswebdesign
Add your company to LinkedIn in just three minutes. - ow.ly/nw1Re

#Tweet19

Videos By Others

Even if you haven't made a video yourself, YouTube and Vimeo have all sorts of videos your target market will find interesting. Do a quick search on those websites and share the link.

> **Taylor Richardson** @EliteInsOK
> Watch to see what Steve Jobs realized that changed everything for him, and can change everything for you. - ow.ly/mrIVs

#Tweet20

Promote Yourself

You shouldn't do this one too often. But every once in a while, feel free to put a tweet out there that's completely and purely promotional. Tell everyone how awesome you are, and how great your products or services are!

Jay D. Parks CPA @jayparkscpa

Thinking about owning your own business? We can help! - ow.ly/jpfOy

#Tweet21

Promote Others

Of course, promoting others is a great idea as well. You build up brownie points with them, and your audience sees that you like to help others out.

> **Golding Group** @GoldingGroup
> @AMAOKC and @ROBYNpromo know how to make a splash with direct mail (yes, this came in the mail): twitpic.com/8wq4r5

#Tweet22

Really Short

Tweet succinctly.

Taylor Richardson @EliteInsOK

Be authentic.

#Tweet23

Email List

Have an email list? Get others to sign up for it by tweeting a link to it. If you don't have a dedicated sign-up page on your website, most email newsletter providers will have a page for you on their site. Make sure to mention why someone would want to sign up for your newsletter.

> **T and S Web Design** @tandswebdesign
> Want online marketing tips in your inbox? Want info on our educational events? Sign up for our newsletter. - ow.ly/gjwnN

#Tweet24

Your Website

Promoting your own website may seem like an obvious idea, but too often people forget to just share the link. Always make sure you give your followers an enticing reason to go to your site when you share it. Or you can share something humorous or interesting about your site.

Golding Group @GoldingGroup
Not sure how the Google search "can you tweet to the president" took someone to our website thegoldinggroup.com but answer is Yes.

#Tweet25

Website Updates

Have you made a major change to your website? Maybe you've added a new page, overhauled an existing one, or redesigned the entire thing. Sounds like something worth sharing!

RococosCrabCake @RococosCrabCake
We have updated the Community page on our website. Check it out sometime: rococo-restaurant.com/community/

#Tweet26

Clients' Websites

Of course, if your clients have websites, it's a great idea to share those as well. Help them to get more eyeballs on their website so people will know what they do. After all, creating more business for them means more business for you.

> **Sandler Training OK** @SandlerOklahoma
> Check out our client and partners new website! - @ComtechDPM: Our NEW website is live
> accesscomtech.com

#Tweet27

Announce New Clients

Did you just land a brand new client? Sounds like a great time to promote them. Take the time to find out if they're on Twitter, so you can tag them. If you can't find them in Twitter's search, be sure to still check their actual website for a link to an official Twitter account.

T and S Web Design @tandswebdesign

We're excited to be helping our new client @jayparkscpa with his social media!

#Tweet28

Retweet a Client

Share something that a client of yours said on Twitter. The Twitter term for that is retweeting. If it's a customer, client, or prospect, it can also serve to remind them of you and help them know, like, and trust you.

Taylor Richardson @EliteInsOK
RT @sandleroklahoma - An effective system lets you recognize and duplicate successful behaviors.

#Tweet29

Retweet Yourself

Have a personal account in addition to your business account? Feel free to retweet something particularly interesting or amusing that you said in that other account. Although you probably have an overlap in followers, the list is most likely not identical. That way more people will see it.

> **Golding Group** @GoldingGroup
> RT @KyleGolding: I just typed "I love market research" in an e-mail and I'm OK with that.

#Tweet30

Retweet Compliments

Did someone pay you a compliment on Twitter? If they tagged you properly, you can find out fairly easily. Depending on your settings, Twitter may even email you. Retweet that compliment for others to see!

RococosCrabCake @RococosCrabCake
Sad, but true! RT @mjnc1980: You know, you'd think a seafood restaurant would rock crab cakes. I guess everyone can't be @RococosCrabCake

#Tweet31

Your Events

Having an open house, client mixer, or meet-up? You can tweet about it! Make sure to include a call to action, and link to any registration page you have set up.

> **Sandler Training OK** @SandlerOklahoma
> Friday is our all-day communication workshop. Find out why you connect naturally with some but not others.

#Tweet32

Educational Events

Do you run workshops or webinars? Or maybe you have a vendor, customer, or client who does. Either way, plug the event, and help spread the word.

T and S Web Design @tandswebdesign

Looking forward to our LinkedIn class this afternoon! - ow.ly/kxRwk

#Tweet33

Networking Events

Are you heading out to a local Chamber event or rotary club meeting? Or maybe you've just returned from a meet-up. Whatever the case, mention it and tag any attendees you're connected with on Twitter.

Golding Group @GoldingGroup

Who will be networking at the @okcchamber Sunset Reception at @CUAOklahoma today?

#Tweet34

Live Events

When you're attending someone else's event, be sure to tweet while you're actually there. If it's an educational event, send out quick tips that you're learning. Make sure to find out if the event has an official hashtag that they recommend you use.

Sandler Training OK @SandlerOklahoma
Watching @Mark_Sanborn at the @NSAOK meeting - he is the author of "You don't have to have a title to be a leader"

#Tweet35

Plug a Nonprofit

Following some local nonprofits? Subscribe to their email newsletter, or just heard about them from somewhere else? Plug them and their mission. When people see your organization isn't selfish, they'll tend to like it even more.

> **Golding Group** @GoldingGroup
> Follow CASA on Twitter @casaofokco. Learn more about how you can make a difference in a child's life.

#Tweet36

Plug the Competition

Not many are brave enough to do this one. Because of that, plugging the competition will make you stand out from the crowd. Share something they do that you don't. Both your competition and your audience will view you differently.

T and S Web Design @tandswebdesign

We know we're not always a good fit for everyone. For another option in the OKC area, check out our friends at www.levanttech.com

#Tweet37

Old Photos

Show people a blast from the past by sharing old photos of your business. Use locations, products, and even people from times past! It's a great nostalgic trip!

RococosCrabCake @RococosCrabCake

Here is a Throw Back Thursday pic of Mr. @Rococos & @AmberKendall to get you into the nostalgics mood for tonight: pic.twitter.com/3d9Jt4L3fp

#Tweet38

Customer Photos

People love to see and share photos of themselves. Make sure you tag them to make it as easy as possible to see it and share it with their friends. And if you don't have any of them, retweet photos they shared.

Golding Group @GoldingGroup
We had a great time at our photo shoot with @Time_Car today. twitpic.com/bil2ii

#Tweet39

Fun Photos

Share fun photos of staff or customers goofing around, having fun, or doing a good deed. It will show more personality than just sharing promotional images.

T and S Web Design @tandswebdesign

8am meeting at @fullcupedmond. A delicious way to start our day. twitpic.com/2zu8vd

#Tweet40

Location Photos

Make it easier to find your location by adding photos. They can be photos of the inside, or of your exterior and the surrounding area. A great time to do this is also when you've just moved into a new place.

Golding Group @GoldingGroup
Since a few people asked, here is a preview pic of the East Coast Office (lot's of work being done right now)
pic.twitter.com/vHP3zzkf2h

#Tweet41

Infographics

Infographics are graphical representations of some sort of info or data. They're typically used to present information in a visual format, where it's easier for people to understand. And people tend to love them, especially well-designed ones! Feel free to share one someone else posted.

T and S Web Design @tandswebdesign
Check out this awesome infographic on the evolution of the web. Hooray for awesome infographics! ow.ly/6KiCb

#Tweet42

Specific Questions

What's the best way to actually get answers? Ask a specific question, rather than a very open-ended question. You can even make it multiple choice, or a yes/no question. This will make others more likely to respond.

Golding Group @GoldingGroup
We like to have fun with our job titles. What your "creative" job title (official or not)?

#Tweet43

You're the Answer

Ask a question where the answer is you! Make it about something that most of your competitors can't (or won't) do, and it will help you stand out from the crowd.

> **Taylor Richardson** @EliteInsOK
> If your house burns down, will your insurance company let you rebuild somewhere else?

#Tweet44

Answer a Question

Of course, other people are asking questions all the time on Twitter. Do a search on key words related to your industry, or just check if anyone had tagged you with a question. Then answer whatever they asked.

RococosCrabCake @RococosCrabCake

@ElwellEats @ChefMeimerstorf @Rococos meatballs today at Penn.

#Tweet45

Ask for Help

None of us can do everything without help. Whether you're looking for advice, recommendations, or instructions, people on Twitter are often able to help out. So feel free to ask for that help!

Taylor Richardson @EliteInsOK
Anyone have vendor suggestions for getting documents signed electronically? So far I'm looking at RightSignature & Docusign.

#Tweet46

Wish for Something

Use Twitter to wish for something that you don't have, that doesn't exist, or that you wish would happen. Often times there's a slightly different solution that you didn't know about. And if you wish for it, people can share that solution with you. At the least, venting every once in a while shows some personality.

T and S Web Design @tandswebdesign
@NETDe Bummer, we wish you could come. We're actually going to have DVDs out before too long.

#Tweet47

Your Opinion

Naturally, you have to be careful with this one. But tweeting what you think about something makes you seem more like a real person, and less like some faceless business.

Jay D. Parks CPA @jayparkscpa
Being the leader God calls you to be as a business owner is a powerful responsibility.

#Tweet48

Make them Think

Ask a question that really makes your reader think. Where are they in their life, and do they want anything more? Are they doing things the right way, or just assuming they are? Make them ponder the deeper things.

> **Taylor Richardson** @EliteInsOK
> Building momentum in your business is like a car going down a hill. Even once you get it going, you still have to steer.

#Tweet49

Challenge a Saying

Use a common saying, then challenge the belief it presents. After all, just because you hear it frequently does not mean that it's actually the truth.

> **Sandler Training OK** @SandlerOklahoma
> Think money doesn't grow on trees? Think again.
> Sandler Rule #11 - Money Does Grow on Trees - ow.ly/n4lfz

#Tweet50

Motivate Them

Motivation is powerful, and it can influence the performance and attitude of others. And it comes off a lot better than being negative and complaining all the time.

Jay D. Parks CPA @jayparkscpa

Success is not a future event! What are you doing to make it happen today?

#Tweet51

Self Deprecating

Don't lower your self esteem, but a little bit of poking fun at yourself, your profession, or your business can make you look a lot more humble. And people usually like humble people a lot better than egotistical people.

> **Taylor Richardson** @EliteInsOK
> Does your insurance agent sound like a drug dealer pushing product, or like a doctor treating a pain?

#Tweet52

Your Products

Have cool stuff for sale? Show it off by actually posting pictures of your products. Let your followers take a look at what you offer, and how awesome it is.

RococosCrabCake @RococosCrabCake
Make no mistake, THIS is what a real crab cake looks like. Only at @Rococos Penn and @Rococo_NP twitpic.com/d3x6ws

#Tweet53

Your Services

Just like products, sharing some of your services can be beneficial. If there's any way to share a photo of you performing the service, maybe with your client, even better!

> **Sandler Training OK** @SandlerOklahoma
> Frustrated with past attempts at improving your management skills? We provide ongoing management training. - ow.ly/k0vgP

#Tweet54

Others' Products

Why stop at promoting your own products and services? Share information on the products of others. It can be something you use at your business, or something a client, business partner, vendor, or just follower sells.

> **Golding Group** @GoldingGroup
> Wow! RT @SamuelGordons: We architected a new cut of diamond. Check out the video explaining what its all about. bit.ly/Tc2la9

#Tweet55

Product Tips

Once you've shared some products that you and others offer for sale, start providing tips. Helpful hints on how to use those products make them that much more useful to your followers. And if they're your products, it's definitely good for business.

T and S Web Design @tandswebdesign

Find out how to create and edit menus in WordPress by watching this video. - ow.ly/ltwqf

#Tweet56

Helpful Tips

There's no need to limit your tips to products, either. Your target market likely has a lot in common. Provide them with tips for things they all do, even if it has nothing to do with products or services you provide. It can be as broad or specific as you want it to be.

Jay D. Parks CPA @jayparkscpa
Getting in arguments? Consider if the other person needs a solution or sympathy.

#Tweet57

Your Awards

Won something lately? Or even been nominated? That's great news! You can tweet once about it, or even share a series of tweets where you tell about the award, and how you won or were nominated for it.

> **Golding Group** @GoldingGroup
> We added some new hardware on our Awards page:
> thegoldinggroup.com/success/awards/

#Tweet58

Thank Retweeters

Did someone retweet something you sent out? You can always thank them for it in a public tweet. And if you're not already following them, definitely do so.

> **Sandler Training OK** @SandlerOklahoma
> @mComputersCRM Thanks for the retweet!

#Tweet59

Thank Others

Of course, people may have done something nice in real life. Whether it was for you, your coworkers, or your business as a whole, be sure to thank them publicly in social media. Unlike a thank you card, that also lets others know how awesome they are!

Jay D. Parks CPA @jayparkscpa

@jonacuff Thanks for a inspiring event in OKC. Enjoyed it very much!

#Tweet60

Compliment Staff

Don't forget to compliment your staff as well. Whether they just completed a great project, made a big sale, or did something outside their comfort zone, be sure to compliment them on Twitter. Everyone should know how great your staff is!

> **Golding Group** @GoldingGroup
> Big shout out this morning for @FeliciteMoorman & @Sean_Hawley making it happen in the great city of Philadelphia. twitpic.com/cqbbju

#Tweet61

New Staff

Hiring a new staff member? Let everyone know by announcing it on Twitter. Of course, if they have a Twitter account, you can also mention them in the tweet, and even add them to a list on Twitter of all your staff.

T and S Web Design @tandswebdesign
Our new programmer, @amber_hanks, is starting this afternoon! We're looking forward to working with her.

#Tweet62

New Products/Services

Have you just got a new product in? Maybe you started offering a new service? Or maybe you're about to start offering a new product or service. Whatever the case, let others know by announcing it on your social media.

Taylor Richardson @EliteInsOK
AARP--Auto & Home Insurance is now available from our agency

#Tweet63

Ebooks

Find a helpful ebook? Or maybe you wrote one yourself? Whatever the case, share the link to the ebook with your followers, whether it's free or paid.

> **Sandler Training OK** @SandlerOklahoma
> Hate traditional selling? Download our ebook to change your view. - ow.ly/n4lfD

#Tweet64

Deadline Reminders

Are their any deadlines associated with services you provide? If so, remind people beforehand in a tweet! It will help them be sure that they're not late, so they're bound to appreciate it.

Jay D. Parks CPA @jayparkscpa
Tax Deadline is looming! File an extension but pay your liability. It is an extension of time to file not to pay!

#Tweet65

Major Holidays

Mentioning something about major holidays is a great topic for tweets. Say something during all the major ones. Of course, this will differ slightly from country to country, and from religion to religion. Make sure you know your target market and keep that in mind.

> **Sandler Training OK** @SandlerOklahoma
> Merry Christmas, everyone, from all of us at Sandler Training!

#Tweet66

Minor Holidays

There's all sorts of weird holidays. Find out what holidays are taking place, and tie them back to you and what your business offers. It can be a great and often humorous way to reference your products and services.

> **Taylor Richardson** @EliteInsOK
> Today is International Panic Day? Of course, if your insurance is set up right, there's no need to panic.

#Tweet67

Birthdays

If you're keeping track of your client's birthdays, be sure to mention those in your tweets as well. Some social networks like Facebook help you keep track of them. But that makes it more impressive when you wish them happy birthday on social networks like Twitter.

RococosCrabCake @RococosCrabCake

Happy Birthday @John_Roy

#Tweet68

Company News

In depth company news can be written up in a blog on your website, then linked to from a tweet. But even shorter tidbits can just be announced completely on the social media website.

Sandler Training OK @SandlerOklahoma
Week #2 in the NEW Sandler Training facility in Oklahoma City – the feedback has been awesome! Thanks to our clients, partners, and fans!

#Tweet69

Industry News

As an expert in your field, you're in a good position to curate content related to your industry. Share news that interests your followers, not just news that interests you. If it will impact them directly, that's a good sign that you should share it with them.

T and S Web Design @tandswebdesign

@LinkedIn recently made changes to their Company Pages. Have you taken these simple steps to optimize yours? - ow.ly/eTVDZ

#Tweet70

Local News

If your organization does a lot of business locally, share local news. It doesn't even have to be directly related to what you do, as long as it's something that affects your local customers.

Taylor Richardson @EliteInsOK
More Hail Storms are coming--not today but it is Oklahoma. If you have Hail Damage on you home and it's not... fb.me/1qft2ppHt

#Tweet71

Vendor News

Your vendors may share news with you on their website, through their social media, or in person. Whatever the case, pass that news along to your followers. Again, make sure it's something that actually impacts them in some way.

T and S Web Design @tandswebdesign
Adobe is stopping Flash development for mobile platforms. Good riddance!

#Tweet72

Your Milestones

Did you just have your most successful week ever? Help the biggest client ever? Do something for the first time? Let your followers know.

RococosCrabCake @RococosCrabCake
Good morning! Less than 12hrs to @Rococo_NP 2.5 Anniversary Party and #RococoCrabCakes announcement. Keep guessing! on.fb.me/12IlVAd

#Tweet73

Twitter Milestones

Hit a big milestone in how many followers your account has? Or maybe the number of tweets you've made? 100? 1,000? 10,000? Announce it to the world!

T and S Web Design @tandswebdesign

2,700 followers! We think that was tweet-worthy. Thank you so much T&S followers, we appreciate your support!

#Tweet74

Start a Hashtag

Hashtags are any word or phrase (with spaces removed) with a # at the beginning. They're used to organize topics and subjects on Twitter. There are a lot of hashtags already in use. So be original, and start your own!

Golding Group @GoldingGroup
Any local media covering @DanGordon and #Dans100k today?

#Tweet75

Twitter Tools

If someone is following you on Twitter, the one thing you can be sure of is that they have a Twitter account. Research and share different Twitter tools that can help them make better use of the social network.

T and S Web Design @tandswebdesign

See a visual map of your Twitter followers with mentionmapp. - ow.ly/muwZG

#Tweet76

Twitter Tips

Some of your followers may be new to Twitter. And even experienced users don't know all the ins and outs. In addition to sharing tools, share some general Twitter tips and tricks as well.

Golding Group @GoldingGroup

Your business or non-profit is on Twitter. You have a plan, right? Have you defined success for your organization?

#Tweet77

Follow Friday

The idea of Follow Friday is that on Fridays, you think of interesting people that you already follow, and recommend that others follow them as well. So the next time you tweet on a Friday, use the hashtag #followfriday and recommend some people to your followers.

RococosCrabCake @RococosCrabCake
#FollowFriday for our TV media friends @DanielleVollmar @LizDueweke @PaulFolger @AshtonEdwards4 @newscowboy @cerretanews

#Tweet78

Other Twitter Accounts

Have more than one Twitter account yourself? You may have a personal one, and you may even have more than one for your business and different products or services you offer. Cross-promote them!

> **Golding Group** @GoldingGroup
> @KyleGolding is presenting to @OKCNewPRPros 4/30/13 bit.ly/11HRXZ5 If this gets 25 RT's he'll give away @Rococos Gift Card @ meeting

#Tweet79

Twitter Lists

Lists on Twitter are a great way of organizing the accounts you follow. Start a list that will interest your followers and share it with them. Or, if you find someone else who is already organizing a great list, share that one.

T and S Web Design @tandswebdesign

Looking for marketing tips on Twitter? Check out this list: twitter.com/mashable/marketing

#Tweet80

Facebook Page

Does your organization have a presence on Facebook as well? Share that link with your Twitter followers. Some of them may be more active on Facebook, so they're more likely to interact with you over there.

RococosCrabCake @RococosCrabCake

Join the Facebook Fan Club: facebook.com/RococoCrabCake

#Tweet81

Google+ Page

Google+ is great if your target market is technology aficionados, or if you just want your website to rank well in search engines. Direct some of your Twitter followers there to build up that audience as well.

> **Sandler Training OK** @SandlerOklahoma
> Have you connected with us on Google Plus? - ow.ly/k0vh5

#Tweet82

Pinterest Board

If you have a board on Pinterest that would interest your followers, share it with them. Or search and find one someone else has created that would interest your followers, and share that.

RococosCrabCake @RococosCrabCake
For all you "Pinners" we just added a Brunch board on our @Pinterest pinterest.com/rococookc/boards/

#Tweet83

LinkedIn Page

LinkedIn is a must if your organization is business-to-business, if you cater mostly to professionals, or if you are in HR. Regardless of the reason for your LinkedIn presence, share the link on Twitter. Feel free to link to both your business page, and your personal profile if appropriate.

Sandler Training OK @SandlerOklahoma

Are you following us on LinkedIn? - ow.ly/kZsx0

#Tweet84

Give Endorsements

Although they're popular on LinkedIn, you can really endorse someone's skills anywhere. Give an endorsement for someone you've done business with. Feel free to endorse both vendors and your clients.

T and S Web Design @tandswebdesign
Your marketing's great, but what do you do when the leads come in? @SandlerOklahoma does an awesome job helping you with that part.

#Tweet85

Share Endorsements

Whether the endorsement originated on Twitter, it was emailed to you, or it was told to you in person, share it! It's okay to shorten a little bit to make it fit. If you find yourself doing too much trimming down, it might be better to wait for a shorter one to come along before you share it on Twitter.

RococosCrabCake @RococosCrabCake
RT @RickMartinOKC: Another great lunch thanks to @Rococos @ChefMeimerstorf !! King Salmon was spot on

#Tweet86

Make Connections

A great way to network is by connecting other people with each other. Even if you don't have something to directly offer either of them, you can make a lasting impression by introducing them.

> **Sandler Training OK** @SandlerOklahoma
> If you are in OKC and not a member of @NWOKC - you should be - just had a visit from Jill the CEO to find out how they can help me!

#Tweet87

Meeting the Famous

Met someone famous lately? Either national, or local? Maybe you ran into them, maybe they actually purchased something from you. Whatever the case, share it online! You can be mysterious, or actually snap a quick picture with them.

RococosCrabCake @RococosCrabCake
Rumor is a few famous legal minds are having lunch at @Rococos right now. #PowerLunch

#Tweet88

Invite Someone Over

Invite someone to come by your store, swing by your office, or meet you for coffee somewhere. Start it on Twitter, but then take it into real life!

T and S Web Design @tandswebdesign

@vintagecoffeeok haha, that would be a lot of coffee! Are you really interested in a site? You should stop by the office!

#Tweet89

Offer Feedback

Many organizations are on Twitter looking for feedback, whether it be on their products, services, branding, customer service, sales, or something else entirely. Share your feedback on how they're doing, especially if it's an organization your target market is likely to be interested in.

> **Sandler Training OK** @SandlerOklahoma
> Watching @timjpriebe with @tandswebdesign deliver an excellent session on Active Social Media for Sales @SandlerOklahoma - great info

#Tweet90

Behind the Scenes

Clients love a peek behind the curtain to see how you do what you do, or just what happens around your workplace. It makes them feel like an insider. So whether it's a short bit of information that's completely on Twitter, or a link to a blog article or YouTube video, give them that glimpse behind the scenes.

T and S Web Design @tandswebdesign

We now have an espresso machine. And a nice one too. Set up a meeting with us and tell us your favorite drink...we'll have it waiting!

#Tweet91

Music Choices

What are you listening to at the office right now? What are your coworkers listening to? Like many other types of tweets, this helps your followers view you as a real person, and not a corporate drone.

Golding Group @GoldingGroup
We decided on classical music in the office today. Really sets a positive mood for strategic planning.

#Tweet92

Plug Your Ads

Plugging your advertising is sort of like meta-advertising. But promoting your appearance in a magazine, on television, or even in a billboard gives you even more exposure.

RococosCrabCake @RococosCrabCake
Have you guys seen the new @rocococaterer ads in OKC publications? Fancy. Give @CateringSam a call.... pic.twitter.com/AYHrsGio33

#Tweet93

Media Mentions

Was there an article written about you recently? Perhaps your organization was on the news, or is about to be. Or maybe it's your client, rather than you. Whatever the case, be sure to plug it in your social media, so more people will be likely to see it. And if the media is hosted online as well, make sure you link to it.

> **Golding Group** @GoldingGroup
> In Your Corner teams up with @Rococos for Fans 4 Oklahoma on.kfor.com/2NJEDUh

#Tweet94

Discounts

If you sell directly to consumers, discounts are somewhat expected when they follow you on Twitter. They're definitely expected if they Like your Facebook Page. Go ahead and share discounts with them. And be sure to occasionally have discounts exclusive to Twitter followers.

RococosCrabCake @RococosCrabCake
Time for #OKARTSDAY @OKArtsCouncil Leadership Arts Happy Hour at @Rococo_NP #ComeHang & get 10% off if you stay for dinner

#Tweet95

Freebies

You can link to freebies without actually having to give away something yourself. Just link to a website that offers some sort of freebies related to your industry that your followers will benefit from.

T and S Web Design @tandswebdesign

Here are 10 sources for web design freebies. - ow.ly/mux0L

#Tweet96

Giveaways

Whether it's a gift card, a scholarship, or food, advertise your giveaways by tweeting about them. Bonus points if you have followers use a hashtag in a tweet to enter to win. And feel free to promote the contests of others!

Sandler Training OK @SandlerOklahoma
Does your non-profit need more high dollar donations? Our scholarship can help. Apply before December 1. - ow.ly/fezjC

#Tweet97

Giveaway Winners

If you give free stuff away by announcing it on social media, it's a no-brainer to use the same social media website to announce the winners as well.

RococosCrabCake @RococosCrabCake

The #RococoCrabCakes winner is @ksearls with a guess of 16,023 on Facebook.

#Tweet98

Plug a Book

Read a good book lately? Think your followers would benefit from reading the book? Let them know how much you liked it. Be sure to link to it on Amazon.com so they can buy it immediately if they'd like to.

> **Taylor Richardson** @EliteInsOK
> Read Seth Godin's call to action about the initiative you're taking... or not taking. - ow.ly/ltu3J

#Tweet99

Goals

One of the best ways to hold yourself and your organization accountable is to share goals you have in public. Social media is a great place to do that, and you can get quick feedback on them as well.

T and S Web Design @tandswebdesign

One of our goals is to add an on-staff copywriter by the end of the year. Anyone know of some good OKC writers who would be interested?

#Tweet100

Resources

Have you found a specific resource helpful? It can be an event, a website, or a local group. Think it would help your followers as well? Share the link with them, so they can start getting the benefit of the tool as well!

Golding Group @GoldingGroup
Cool trade show in OKC: Party & Event Expo, from backyards to ballrooms – the ultimate resource for any gatherings! buff.ly/18KUmYP

#Tweet101

Customer Service

Some bigger organizations have a Twitter account completely dedicated to providing customer service. Use your main account to provide some customer service, and you'll be going above and beyond what most organizations do.

> **Taylor Richardson** @EliteInsOK
> If you're a client of Elite Insurance and you've been affected by the tornado today, please call us immediately so we can help 405-241-9710

#Tweet102

Right Now

Share what you're doing right now. No, really. Right now. This very second.

Your Account @YourUsername

Whatever you're doing right now...

Want More Advice?

Frustrated with your online marketing efforts?

Worried that you're wasting your time marketing online?

Sign up for the free T&S email newsletter and receive ongoing helpful online marketing advice.

tandsgo.com/newsletter

Connect With Us

Twitter: @102tweetsBook

Facebook: facebook.com/102tweets

Thanks!

Special thanks to everyone that made this book possible. Thanks to my wife, Leann Priebe, who makes everything I do possible, and supports me through all my wacky projects.

Thanks to the T&S clients who we manage social media for for giving me the experience I needed to put together 102 individual tweets. Thanks to all the organizations and people that let us use their tweets in the book: Elite Insurance Associates, Golding Group, Jay D. Parks, CPA, Rococos, Sandler Training of Oklahoma.

And special thanks to Holly Titus, who didn't believe I would write this book, thereby motivating me to get it done. Take that, Holly.

Finally, thanks to you, my reader. Now start tweeting!

Made in the USA
Monee, IL
04 November 2026

67379796R00065